Write, publish, and promote a non-fiction book to market your business

from

IDEA TO AUTHOR-ITY®

Dixie Maria Carlton

First Published 2014
Fifth Edition Published 2025 by Dixie Maria Carlton

Published by Dixie Carlton Limited
www.dixiecarlton.com
New Zealand

Produced by Indie Experts Publishing & Author Services
www.indieexpertspublishing.com

Copyright © Dixie Maria Carlton 2025

All rights reserved.

The moral right of the author to be identified as the author of this work has been asserted.

Apart from any fair dealing for the purposes of study, research or review, as permitted under the copyright act, no part of this book may be reproduced by any process without written permission of the author.

Every effort has been made to trace and acknowledge copyright material; should any accidental infringement have occurred, the author tends her apologies.

Product and other names used herein may be trademarks of their respective owners. The author disclaims any and all rights associated with those marks.

Disclaimer:
Every effort has been made to ensure this book is as accurate and complete as possible. However, there may be mistakes, both typographical and in content. Therefore, this book should be used as a general guide and not the definitive source for the kind of information contained herein. The author and publisher shall not be liable or responsible to any person or entity with respect to any loss or damage caused or alleged to have been caused directly or indirectly by the information contained in this book.

Cover design by Daniela Catucci
Typesetting & Layout by Ammie Christiansen, Fast Forward Design
Typeset in 11pt Minion Pro

ISBN
Printed: 978--0-6481295-8-5

For Alex

Contents

Introduction		7
1	Planning and Writing Your Manuscript	11
2	Finishing the First Draft	17
3	Pre-Press and Production	21
4	Book Design	27
5	How to Get and Use Great Reviews	33
6	Printing Options	37
7	The Publishing Industry	49
8	Self-Publishing Your Book	51
9	Publicity	55
10	Distribution	63
11	Talk it up: From Pages to Stages	69
12	Online Marketing Options	73
13	Social Media	83
14	Pulling it All Together	85
Bonus Chapter: Using WordPress as Your Website Platform		89
About Dixie Maria Carlton		96
This Is Just the Beginning		98
Other Books from Dixie Maria Carlton		99

Introduction

"You just don't know what you don't know... yet!"

I love this saying because it captures exactly the mysterious journey that lies ahead for first-time authors on the path to becoming an '*author*-ity'.

I'm not sure why I'm still surprised when new writers say things like 'But this is such a great book. How do I get it onto Amazon?', or 'I just have to get an agent and then the rest will be easy', or words to that effect. Another one I constantly come across is the author who thinks that the easier option will be to simply create an e-book instead of a 'real' book.

Even the original version of this book was intended to be 'just an e-book', but there are a million books of all varieties abandoned on computers and in landfills that attest to the fact that any kind of book still needs to be properly written, edited, formatted, designed and then marketed. That's before you even get to the issue of distribution.

The hard truth is, a number of authors have already written about *your* subject – some good and some bad, some wealthy ones and many who are now sadly sitting on the boxes of their unsold books instead of furniture. There are no new ways to become wealthy, paths to enlightenment or management techniques. They are mostly the same as someone else's version of it but told with fresh stories or examples. The world is not waiting for *your* words – sorry. But if you have the wherewithal to back yourself and your message and turn your material into a book (either digital or printed) and do it well, then you have a chance at getting your book looked at seriously by any number of publishers, agents or booksellers. You just have to know how the system works – from idea to finished product – and then how to get it out to your market.

Some people do fluke it. But even the most successful authors often received enough rejection slips to wallpaper a small office before finally hitting the literary jackpot. I don't believe in fluking it. You really have to be exceptionally good (or know someone who knows someone – *wink, wink*) to be able to bypass the alligator-filled moats and traverse the drawbridges that protect most publishing castles.

Note: Celebrities – especially of the culinary or sporting kind – are a whole other story!

So, what do you need to know about publishing in order to have a real shot at making it?

Here's a list of 10 things – but these are 10 out of 100 and just the basics. These rules are the same whether you work with a traditional publisher, you self-publish, or you want to do e-books.

1. Get a good book editor to go through your manuscript and make sure it is AWESOME, not just 'pretty good'.
2. Work with a book shepherd or industry specialist who knows how to get the book from manuscript to 'ready for publishing', whether that means ready to self-publish or ready to submit to a traditional publisher.
3. Know who your target market is, why they would want to buy your book, and what they might pay for similar books

on the same subject.

4. Find out who else is writing (well) about your subject.
5. Have a reason for writing the book – not just an idea you can make money as a writer. (Most likely you won't!)
6. Be prepared to speak about and promote your book yourself – your publishers won't do a lot, unless you are paying them to and/or you are already very famous and selling millions.
7. Learn how to sell from the platform and use public relations and social media to get your book promoted.
8. Join some relevant associations and submit articles and blogs to their magazines or websites, so that you can attract some direct attention for your book from those already interested in your topic; i.e., your target market.
9. Create a website and make sure it's professional and geared towards promoting your book and your expertise as an author and speaker, so that people can go there to find out more about buying your book and/or tapping into your expertise in other ways (beyond your book).
10. Learn how to creatively position yourself in your market, to promote your work within your genre. Get smart about your personal marketing and personal brand.

Working with an agent is likely to happen only if you have really outstanding ideas, quality material and a very well-prepared manuscript or a completed book which already has a track record of sales.

A big publisher is likely to look at your work only if you can get their attention, and that means having a great agent who loves your work and will promote you well, or a book which is topping the charts already.

If you are a new author, you owe it to yourself to learn all you can about how this industry works, how other authors have succeeded, and what's made some books standout successes in your genre.

I first wrote this book back in 2011 for all the authors who were embarking on their journey to write and publish a book. But even in the last 10 or 15 years the publishing world has changed significantly, and so this updated edition is now based on the knowledge I've gained from the more than 200 books (mostly nonfiction) I've published, nurtured or coaxed into life since 2006.

I sincerely wish you use this information to assist you in getting your book from inside your head into the hands of your market, easily.

Dixie

PS: When you finish this book, scoot over to my website, where you'll find lots of great resources, downloadable tools and more. Details are at the end of this book.

Planning and Writing Your Manuscript

Start with WHY

Before you even pick up a pen or plug your laptop in, you need to get some clarity about why you are writing a book in the first place. What is driving you to commit to weeks or months of planning, writing, preparation, and production? Please spend some time thinking through these very important questions...

- *Why* do you want to write this book?
- Why *this* book, and why *now*?
- What do you want to have happen as a result of writing it?
- What call to action can you include in the book to ensure 'something happens' for you, for your readers...?

Your answers might include:
- *Make money from sharing my knowledge.*
- *Use this book to attract new clients and speaking opportunities.*

The answers to these questions will be different for each one of us. So, first things first: grab a big sheet of paper, some (coloured) pens, and ask yourself the big questions below.

Get really clear on your answers. You might come up with a dozen or more for each of the questions. That's great! The more answers you have, the better. Then, when you have written them all down, sit on the Q&As for a full day and night. Maybe even longer. See what else comes up for you as you mull this over.

Meditate on it, talk it over with your best friend or partner, and then review again...

- Why do you *really* want to write a book?
- What do you *really* want to have happen for you/your business as an author?
- What action do you *really* want people to take after reading your book?

Now put those answers somewhere you'll see them every day. Keep this 'WHY' top of mind throughout the writing process.

Planning Your Book

Here's one easy way to lay out the book so that your content flows easily from one subject to another.

Start with a blank piece of paper and map out the following grid.

(Even if you are not specifically going to have your book divided into parts 1–3, these give you a framework for where each part of your book might go.)

Write up what each 'part' is about. Then, decide what the three main chapters in each part will be about. Using the same example, your Part 2 (Marketing) look like this: Chapter (4) Traditional marketing; Chapter (5) Online marketing; and Chapter (6) Customer services. This then segues smoothly into Part 3: People. Chapter (7) therefore might be about the importance of hiring the friendliest and most helpful people for the front line of your business.

PLANNING AND WRITING YOUR MANUSCRIPT

For example, if you are writing a self-help book about small business, the first part would be about accounting, the second part about marketing, and the third part about hiring staff.

Introduction			
Part 1 *Accounting*	Chapter 1 *Accounting Software*	Chapter 2 *Business Planning*	Chapter 3 *Tax Management*
Part 2 *Marketing*	Chapter 4 *Traditional Marketing*	Chapter 5 *Online Marketing*	Chapter 6 *Customer Service*
Part 3 *Employees*	Chapter 7 *Finding People*	Chapter 8 *Keeping People*	Chapter 9 *Firing People*
Summary			

Write the working chapter headings into each of the squares of the grid.

You may end up with three chapters for each part, with a short introductory chapter for each (i.e., a total of 12 chapters), or you might have only nine chapters, and each might be separated as 'Part 1, Part 2, Part 3'.

You may also find that your book ends up being 15 chapters (ie 5 short chapters for each of the three parts). It will depend on you and your content. This plan allows you to get an idea of that framework before you start writing. It will also give you a clear outline of how the book will flow when it's finished.

Please don't overthink it at this stage, as it's firstly about getting the ideas out of your head as a framework for this book that's currently bouncing around in your head.

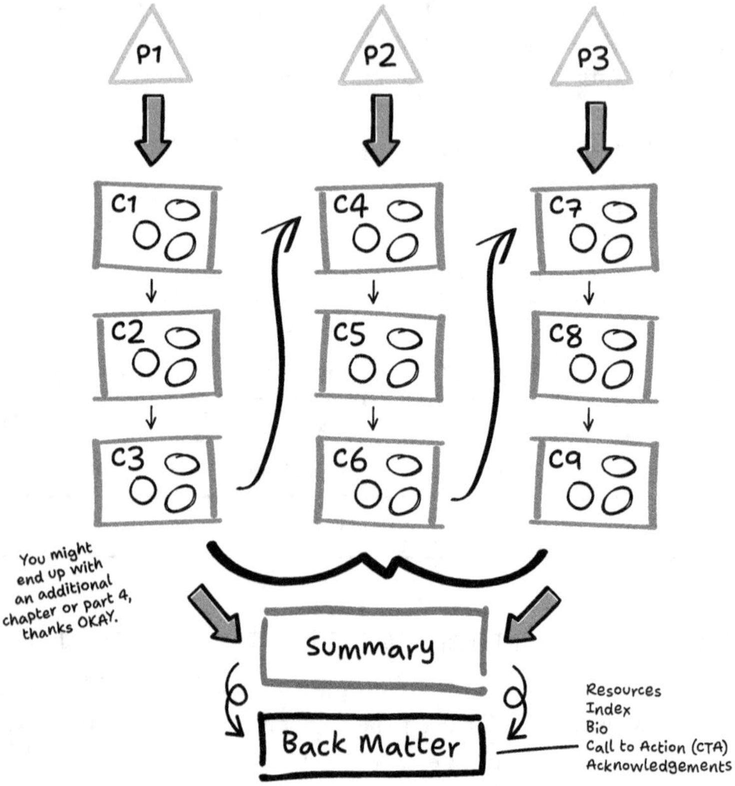

For a full breakdown of all the ways to use this method, please check out the first book in this series – *Start With the Draft*. There you'll find specific resources, worksheets and more to help you maximise your ideas through a solid planning process that will lead to a well thought out book plan.

It's a variation on a typical mind-map. But this works to organise your mind map branches.

Let me explain.

Many people who like to work with lists also love the concept of a Mind Map – where you start with one point, then take that into various branches and subbranches with ideas over a massive sheet of paper. You might connect some of those branches up and then end up with a clear idea of all the content you want to write about, but still it's fragmented.

Using this framework as outlined above, means you can then take the main branches of your mindmap, put them into some order and further order their respective sub-branches so that the writing phase is made easier.

I call this the Tri-Variant Framework™ and I've literally helped hundreds of authors to write their books using this as a starting point.

One other thing: don't write your book in chronological order. Instead, select which chapter you wish to write next – I recommend tackling the easy ones first. Once you get to the halfway mark, it will feel easier to keep going and finish your manuscript. If you started at chapter one then get to chapter three and find particularly hard or needs a lot of research, then by the time you finish it and still have seven more chapters to go, you may well feel de-motivated to carry on. But if you left those tediously long or laborious ones till last, you'll know that you've nearly finished anyway.

This grid system is also helpful when working with other authors on joint projects. You can all decide on the general layout of the chapters, and then select who will write each one, agreeing to swap them over when finished to check (and add to) each other's work.

Do NOT start writing until you have the plan in place. Often someone will come to me with a completed manuscript, and some big parts are too long and some too short, or the readability and flow is lacking.

Ideally, you will end up with each chapter having about three or four subheadings, and each of those will be 600–800 words long. This means each chapter is going to be somewhere between 1,800 and 2,500 words, and your book will be anything from 24,000 to 35,000 words.

This translates to 120–160 pages depending on layout, graphics and images used. If you can commit to writing 2,000 words per week, you'll have your first draft completed within three to four months.

Need an SOS?

Feeling overwhelmed? Uncertain about your next move? Whether you're just starting out or stuck somewhere in the messy middle, Dixie and the team of **experts** at Indie Experts Publishing are here to guide you—every step of the way.

This is your **Support On Standby**—ready when you are.

Let's make publishing simple: *www.indieexpertspublishing.com*

Finishing the First Draft

You're nearly there. The writing is now completed, and while there may be some revisions and updates required after your editor has gone through your manuscript, you are now at the stage of preparing to print your book. However, it's not just a matter of taking a Word file to your printer. There's still work to be done.

Review Content and Get Feedback

Once you have completed the preliminary draft of your manuscript, that's the best time to turn it over to someone else to take a good look at it. That person will be someone who is a professional in the publishing field, maybe publishing coach, book shepherd or editor.. They should be able to give you some good early feedback on your content. What you are looking for at this stage is *completion of content*. Then you will also need some test pilots (also known as beta readers). A small group of friendly people – either friends, associates or even a client or two – to read through and give you some feedback on their findings about your book being reader friendly, on point, lacking too much jargon, or identifying where they get stuck.

If you are co-authoring a book, select which parts you will focus on first, write those, and then swap over so that the other person can review and add content as needed to each section.

With all that feedback, you can go back and complete what you need to add in to your manuscript, give it another good review yourself and then hand it over for editing.

Edit content

A formal edit, using a good professional *book* editor, will highlight any discrepancies in your text such as repetitive or missing information, errors, what needs to be referenced, and whether your text is readable and flows.

Your editor will often make any needed corrections and then highlight the comments or areas that you need to re-do or sort out before they give the manuscript back to you for finishing. You may need to repeat this process, depending on how much your editor has recommended changing or updating.

This is not a final edit – there are likely to still be many errors and things to correct before your book is ready for printing – so don't worry too much about spelling mistakes or missed commas at this stage. Just continue to correct anything that needs to be fixed and ask anyone else who might also be checking your manuscript to do so with a red pen or highlighter.

Before the book is handed over to the pre-press department, the manuscripts (and however many copies there are) will have corrections that need to be updated and checked off in a final copy. The easier you can make this process the better, and using pencil or black ink can be harder to spot on a printed file than coloured pens and highlighters.

Finalize Content

Check your manuscript yet again and then, when you are *completely* happy that it is finished in terms of content and that most of the grammar and spelling checks have been done, it's time to sign off on the manuscript and get it to the pre-press stage.

This whole process may take as little as four weeks, or as long as a year – depending on your own need to keep re-writing (trust me, it happens more than you'd imagine) and your editing team. I say 'team' because there is more than one kind of editor involved at this stage.

Copy Editor

A copy editor reviews the content in raw form, advising on readability, mistakes, and references required. From there, a reasonable amount of re-writing or updating may be required.

Proofing Editor

This person is more likely to pick up all errors, closely review the grammar and spelling, and polish the contents.

Final Proofing

This needs to be done by a *completely* fresh pair of eyes – after the book has come back from the pre-press stage of being typeset. Sometimes, the typesetting may result in an occasional word being dropped or repeated, or formatting errors being introduced. Final proofing is best done by someone who is not a copy editor because often a copy editor will want to contribute more thoughts on reworking parts of your book, and you should be well past having to make those decisions at this stage.

Pre-Press and Production

Check references and then double-check them for accuracy and consistency in the way they are presented.

Illustrations and Diagrams

Determine what illustrations, diagrams, photos or coloured images need to be included, and where they will go. Do you need someone else to create them for you? If so, what style will they be in? You have options of hand-drawn illustrations, clip art (not recommended), photos and what you can find on the internet.

Beware of copyright issues related to use of images and diagrams. If you want to use photos from the internet, check what you are and are not allowed to use. If you have commissioned something to be created or photographed for you and have paid for that, then you own the images. But if you are using something from any other source, there could be copyright restrictions, such as where you use them, how you use them, limited publication rights and more. Pay close attention to the fine print when you download something you think you've paid for. Take, for example, the author who really liked an image he used for his book cover, only to find out after it was published that if he sold more than a certain number of books, he would have to pay a *lot* more for the use of that image.

If you have created diagrams and special images which are

particularly relevant to your work but could easily be used by other people, then it's worth talking to an intellectual property lawyer about obtaining trademarks and extra copyright protection.

You own your material and therefore automatically own the copyright to it. However, there are precautions you can take to ensure that someone on the lookout for what you have created is further restricted (or at least thinks twice about it) from just taking it and using it as theirs. As stated before, if you have any doubts or questions about intellectual property, seek out a good intellectual property lawyer.

Foreword

A foreword is what you ask someone else to write as an introduction to your book. An introduction is usually written by you, as a preface to the contents and to outline what the book is about. Also, note that this is spelled as 'fore' with an 'e' – a commonly misspelled word that it would be embarrassing to get wrong in your book.

Writing a foreword is considered an honour by most people, and you want to be sure you ask a strongly relevant person to do this for you. Be selective. Ask yourself 'why this person' and be sure you know the answer. Some people, when they know you are writing a book, will offer to write a foreword and they may not be the best option.

Someone who is closely associated with the topic and has some weight and credibility within the industry is your best choice. Avoid having this be merely 'someone famous'. For example, a book about raising children may have a better foreword by the Children's Commissioner, or the mother of eight children, than Oprah Winfrey.

Introduction

An introduction is not to be confused with a preface or foreword. It may be that you also ask someone to write an introduction for your book, but more commonly you will write this yourself. Your introduction will be a 500–1,500-word summary about what the book will cover and the sorts of things addressed in the various chapters, so that the reader knows what to expect. A preface and epilogue are generally found in fiction books and are pre-story pieces.

It is not necessary to have an introduction or a foreword, and many books have neither or only one or the other. This comes down to the author's preference, although some editors will suggest the need for an introduction based on their perception of how easily the reader may get into the book without one.

Dedication

Most books have a dedication. This is the couple of lines where you thank your mother, spouse, children, or inspirational person for their input or for being part of your life in some way. This is usually not more than one or two lines. The dedication goes at the front of the book, just before the contents page.

Acknowledgements

The acknowledgements are what you might think of as your 'Award Acceptance Speech'. This might be one or even two pages of thank you messages to those people who helped in some way to get your book written and produced. You may like to thank your spouse or significant other family member(s) for giving you the encouragement or the peace and quiet to write, but you are also most likely to use this space to thank the researchers, editors, sounding board people, mentors, employees, your business partner(s) or coach. Be generous with your praise here, and don't forget the important people who did contribute to your book in various ways.

You should also thank the reviewers of your book here, those who went through it and gave you feedback – both the formal and informal reviews. (See Reviews section).

Disclaimer

The world is filled with people who like to write challenging feedback on everything from political speeches to rising prices, and so there may well be someone who fronts up with some feedback on your book one day, who takes delight in pointing out a misspelled word on page 63, or who considers your advice to be all they think they need to change their lives or revolutionise their business. It is therefore important to add a disclaimer which absolves you from responsibility for any reader's interpretation of your work. The disclaimer is the paragraph inside your book which explains that:

Every effort has been made to ensure it is as accurate and complete as possible; however, there may still be errors, both typographical and in content. The author and the publisher shall not be held liable or responsible to any person or entity with respect to any loss or damage caused or alleged to have been caused directly or indirectly by the information contained in this book.

(This is a fairly standard disclaimer used on many nonfiction publications. You are welcome to use this example as for your own book.)

This should be more than enough to prevent anyone from trying to sue you or your publisher for action the reader may take as a result of your shared wisdom which might result in their business taking a downturn or their children or pets not behaving in a certain way etc. This states that you have checked your facts (and you most definitely should have) and the reader's interpretation of the contents is their own – not your – responsibility.

Table of Contents

Ideally keep your table of contents to one or two pages only. You may have lots of great subtitles for each chapter, but consider for

example if I'd used subtitles as part of this book's table of contents, then it would be six pages long. Remember, people want to *get into the book*. The table of contents is helpful for anyone wanting to just dip in to sections, but your subheadings throughout each chapter will make it easy for readers to find specific sections within chapters.

Glossary

A glossary is an alphabetical listing of terms and their meanings at the back of your book. The glossary is **especially important in the case of technical translations and marketing books and should be used for any local or industry jargon too.**

Index

An index lists terms, names and themes you mention throughout the book, and which pages they are found on. For example, you may have mentioned 'depression' throughout a book on mental health, and it would appear in the index as follows:

depression – 12, 15, 46, 47, 48, 65, 81, 91

medicating depression – 12, 46, 48, 91

You may choose to list the main word only, but in some very technical books, your readers may appreciate the extension too.

Some programs will create an index for you automatically; however, we recommend leaving the creation of your index to the very last of your tasks, and that you check the references are all correct. It is one job best left to fact checkers and those with a love of detail.

An important point: You will also need to triple check page numbers referenced throughout your book too as items can appear on different page numbers as edits are made, text is shifted around, or diagrams inserted – and for this reason, it's vital to check the Table of Contents still lists the correct page numbers too.

About the Author

This is the part where you profile yourself, your business, and/or your ongoing availability for the reader and how they can reach you. Include your website, social media sites, and services you provide in this part of your book.

Remember: the main reason for writing a book is to profile your knowledge and experience as an expert to your market, so use this page (or two pages) very well and put your best marketing foot forward. If you are uncomfortable writing promotional copy about yourself, this is an excellent time to hire a professional copywriter.

Book Design

Internal Layout

While all these things are being done, your book will be in the hands of one of the most important people of all – the designer and typesetter. This may be one or two people. Some designers also take care of the typesetting; in some cases, the designer is a separate person altogether. For the sake of simplicity, I'm going to refer to them as being one person and refer to them collectively as 'the designer'.

Finding a good designer is important. There are some aspects of book design that are quite different for magazines and websites or other forms of graphic design. Your book designer needs to have some skills and experience with the book industry and know how to create a great cover – and that often means being able to get a feeling for the book itself and understand its target readership and therefore how to reach them visually.

One great place to source a good designer and also see samples of their work is online. For example, on the website www.Fivrr.com, various service providers such as designers can link up with potential clients and arrive at an agreed price and terms of business. You pay for what you get once you're happy with the work. It's usually very affordable, and reliable.

Fonts and Internal Layout

There are great books, average books, and some that are just plain ugly and hard to read. I'm talking about the aesthetics of the insides of a book. Your choice of font, size and range of headings, margins, and headers can all contribute to making a book easy and reader friendly. Wrong choices will create something that most people have to really work hard at reading and therefore struggle to enjoy.

Whether you have attended a concert or a pottery class, it's the smooth running of the show (along with the content) that makes it something you'll enjoy. It's the same with books.

Here are some ways to achieve this:

- Avoid pages of unbroken paragraphs. Break them up with subheadings.
- Add diagrams, images or illustrations to make your book interesting visually.
- Put quotes into a special space, bigger text, and/or in italic fonts so that they stand out.
- If you have a special information or excerpts, put them into consistently formatted boxes or shaded background blocks.
- Ensure a reasonable amount of white space, with text not going too close to the edge of the pages.
- Place easy-to-identify chapter headers at the top of each page.
- Don't mix your fonts and size of text up too much. Stick with simple, clean, easy-to-read, easy-on-the-eye styles of text.
- The font for your regular text should be 10–12 point, depending on the one you choose. Avoid small font sizes, as this can be frustrating even for people with good eyesight. Better to have slightly larger type than too small and spread the spacing between lines and paragraphs well. It's preferable to have

a higher page count than squash your text up to save paper. Your readers will thank you for this.

Engaging a professional book designer will help to ensure you don't get someone testing silly and unworkable – 'but gorgeous' – styles in your book. Some designers get carried away. That's fine in magazines and brochures, but not books – unless it is a very 'creative' style of book and subject and that is your point of difference.

Less is more when it comes to book formatting in most instances.

A point of difference for some books is that they are designed to be highly visual, with lots of break out colours, boxes of big ideas, highlighted points in what I call Creative 3D. If that's what you're aiming for, then that's a whole different matter and maybe a magazine designer is a good option. But remember to go back to who your market is, how you want to reach them and have them react after reading your book. If your book is big, boldly colourful, therefore also more expensive and not something that leads your readers to a conclusion that you or your company can assist them to resolve their problems, then consider again the entire purpose of writing and producing this book.

I've seen utterly delicious looking books that you just want to pick up and take home and put on your coffee table, but that never really end up being read properly.

A boldly colourful and creative book also may not work so well for you as a downloadable eBook – and again you need to consider your target market. How do they want their information? eBooks, Audio books, print versions of these in various formats might need to be considered for all the ways you really want your book to work for you.

Start with the end in mind when planning your book and you'll resolve these issues easily.

Front Cover

Some book covers are as minimalist as bold text against a plain background, and others include photos or diagrams. Different styles of cover will appeal differently. There is an art to this. In some cases, it takes a lot of trial and error to get the best cover; in other cases, the right cover will be the one a great designer comes up with first. I've known some books where half a dozen covers have been tested before, finally, 'the best one' just happened; at other times, it's been a case of *'thanks – the first cover was brilliant'*, and we went no further in the testing or design phase. Every cover is different – but having an experienced book designer definitely helps.

The best way to get your cover design sorted is to find out what you like in other books and then discuss this with a professional *book* designer who can cater to your requests. Don't ask an inexperienced designer to play with something they think is 'cool'. Remember, your cover is the first sales pitch for your book and needs to reflect the content, as well as be bold and inviting.

When you are happy with one or two designs, test them on a selection of your target market. This may mean standing on the street for half an hour at a couple of locations and asking people to give you feedback and state their preference. Get them to tell you what they both do and don't like about the options. Don't say you are the author, as often they won't tell you what you really need to hear, or you end up engaged in time-consuming discussions about writing books that distract you from your particular mission – to ask as many people as possible for feedback on your cover design(s).

If standing on a street corner is not your idea of a fun way to do market research, don't worry. Now you have options with social media and your own data base of contacts you can run polls with. But while asking real people in a live situation is perhaps an old-fashioned option in this digital age, don't discount it if you can get a group of people together somewhere and ask them.

Book clubs, the coffee shop, your business networking breakfast group are all options for doing this.

Back Cover

Unless it's the latest 'hot book' that everyone is raving about it, your readers will want to read the back cover to reassure themselves that they wish to buy the book, so this is another element to get right.

Description

The description should include a subheading at the top, very well written 'sales' copy of one or two paragraphs, some bullet points, and a couple of brief raves about it from prominent reviewers. You may also like to ensure a small piece near the barcode and ISBN that specifies the genre, so that when your book is being stocked in the shelves of a library or bookstore, there is no confusion as to where it should be. For example, a book with the title of *Escaping Quicksand* might be about either avoiding bankruptcy (financial self-help), working smarter (business nonfiction), tramping in the great outdoors (outdoor adventure), or it could be a crime novel. You can't rely on salespeople to know where it goes unless they have the time and/or presence of mind to read the back cover, and they often don't have either.

A good back cover looks clean, is well written and is not cluttered with too much information. Engage someone with experience to help with this if you are unsure. *It's well worth getting it right!*

International Standard Book Numbers

International Standard Book Numbers (ISBNs) are a cataloguing tool used worldwide to identify every book published. These are obtainable from the national libraries in most countries, and are *free* in NZ and Australia, but charged for in many countries now.

You simply call, email or apply online to ask for one. Google ISBN Numbers for your country to get the best option. It will either be through a company such as Bowker Thorpe, or a National Library. You may have to describe your book project so that the correct type of number is issued, and if you are a publisher or are planning to produce several books, you may request blocks of numbers.

ISBNs are unique to each book in the world, and your responsibility in having an ISBN is to ensure at least two copies of your book are sent to the National Library in the country of ISBN issue for cataloguing. This also ensures that your book is registered on the Global Register of Publishers database, so that it can be located by anyone in the world who might have a particular interest in your subject.

You may also be surprised to find that your ISBN is not only unique to your book but enables it to be searched by the international network of libraries all over the world. Once a book is in the ISBN system, it is searchable anywhere by this unique identification number, and publishers take great care to ensure each book is carefully catalogued.

If you are uploading your book for sale to Amazon or Ingram Spark, you can also request a free ISBN from them during that process. However, be advised that these ISBNs are for sales on those platforms only. I rcommend getting your own ISBNs.

Barcode

A barcode can be issued against the ISBN by your printer on request and usually costs well under $100. Your printer will often be able to supply your barcode.

If you are producing your book with Kindle they can supply both the ISBN number and the barcode for you if required.

How to Get and Use Great Reviews

A couple of years ago, I was publishing a book for a man we'll call Allan. He got all enthusiastic and sent his nearly finished book off to someone he knew reasonably well, someone who had some minor celebrity status, and, in Allan's view, was therefore a great person to have rave about his book. He was very excited about the feedback he got from this man and decided his testimonial was perfect for the back cover.

When asked to check that his associate was happy with the way we'd put his words on the back cover (a final check before printing), to Allan's surprise and embarrassment the man said that he hadn't realised Allan was going to do that. He said that the feedback he'd emailed to him was for Allan's personal use, not to be bandied about. And he advised that due to an upcoming issue that was going to be reported negatively about his business in the press, Allan might well prefer to not have his friend's raving endorsement for this particular book.

This awkwardness happens a lot. Another thing that trips up the review process is giving your finished manuscript to someone – after it's all been laid out and is looking lovely – and they don't understand that you only want a comment or quote about the book, not suggestions for a rewrite!

Six steps to getting great reviews for your book:

1. Decide who you want to review it – and then understand that asking 20 people does not mean *all* of them will respond. It's worth aiming for 3–6 reviews. If you get more than that, then use the not quite so glowing or powerful ones on the book's website and marketing platforms. A powerful endorsement quote is not necessarily going to come from Oprah or Tony Robbins or any other top-ranked celebrities just because you know them. The best ones will come from those who have relative professional positions, or other books, which means they are well qualified to comment. For example, a book about child safety with an endorsement from the Minister of Child Services or a Family Court judge may carry far more weight than Tony Robbins in the minds of the readers anyway.

2. Ask them if they would be willing to review your book. Be sure they know that you intend to use their comments – and possibly in condensed or edited format – for marketing purposes, and that may include being quoted on the book cover itself.

3. Set a timeline by which you need their response.

4. Provide a list of pre-prepared short quotes – you can write some examples yourself - and invite them to either use any of those you've supplied or to take them as inspiration for their own words. This makes it so much easier for people who do struggle to find the right thing to say, or to understand the type of thing you require.

5. Get it in writing that your reviewers expect no payment for this endorsement, and that they will accept your right to edit their comment.

6. *Send them a signed copy of your book when it's printed.*

This system of getting reviews can make it easy for other authors, celebrities, or experts to agree to review your book. When used correctly, this can save you the embarrassment of printing comments about your book that are not signed off on, or whose purpose is misunderstood by the reviewer.

Printing Options

Before your book is ready for printing, you will need to assess your options. You can have it printed in a traditional sense – paper and ink; hard copy or paperback – or you may wish to create an e-book or audio book. And there's even more to it than that. The first part of the process is determining exactly how to get it into the hands of your prospective readers, by knowing who they are and in what format they would prefer to have your book.

Many people love having their books on readers such as Kindle or iPad. Just as many want to pick up and thumb through old-fashioned pages. You can do both – you are not limited to only one option here. But let's look at these options in more detail, and help you to understand what you need to do for each.

e-Books

Producing an e-book is more than just typing something up on your laptop and saving it as a PDF file. An e-book still needs to be edited, typeset, designed, a cover created, and an ISBN issued. In fact, the only thing that really separates a quality printed book from a quality electronic book is how it's delivered to the reader – online or on paper.

Some might think that taking shortcuts on e-books is acceptable, but seriously, if you have gone to the trouble of writing a good book, edited it, ensured it's looking good and of high quality in either style, then it's worth doing a good job of the final production phase. And not only will your readers appreciate the time taken to do so, but your quality publication will stand out above others that look like the poor relations by comparison.

You can, of course, produce your e-book by turning it into a PDF file, but for it to have wider appeal to your market, you'll want to have it converted into files suitable for a range of electronic *readers*. The reason for converting into an e-reader-friendly option is so that the book automatically fits the size of the e-reader, and the pages flow easily and at the right sizes as requested by the reader of your book.

Convert to EPUB

There are various software options and online websites where you can simply upload your text, word or PDF file and have it converted to an EPUB file, which can then be read by Apple iPad, Barnes and Noble NOOK, Kindle, Sony Reader, BeBook, Adobe Digital Editions, Lexcycle Stanza, AZARDI, Aldiko, WordPlayer on Android and the Mozilla Firefox add-on OpenBerg Lector. The ones most common at the time of writing are the **iPad, Kindle, and Barnes & Noble NOOK**. Others come and go – but these are the ones most likely to be used by your target market.

There are also specialist e-book distributors online and printed book outlets, specializing in particular genres such as fiction or non-fiction, (and even some stores now who specialize in subcategories such as horror romance, military, paranormal, or business books, etc) and these may be of interest to you. However, remember why you are writing a book and who you wish to target.

For the purposes of reaching your target market and ensuring they understand your specialist knowledge and services, the option you are most likely to choose is to convert your book to an EPUB file.

If you do wish to convert to an EPUB version, I recommend getting help from someone who is an expert at this.

The cost of converting your book to an EPUB file is likely to be anything from zero to several hundred dollars, depending on how much customization is necessary, and whether you are comfortable using online resources and software for this yourself.

One of the things that's changed a lot in the past few years is how easy it is now to upload your books to Amazon via Kindle Direct Publishing (KDP).

If you are creating an e-book version of your book, ensure that you do embed relevant hyperlinks and images, perhaps even video and audio files. These bring additional flavour and value to your book.

Print Books

Printing your book on paper is still a very good idea for most nonfiction books, and here's why:

- They are more easily shared and lent to friends and associates.
- More than any other format, print books are likely to be kept, along with notes and highlights inserted by the reader.
- Print books are more easily sold or handed out as a tangible item *of value* when marketing your services.

One thing that might work very well for you is to offer a printed book and make the e-book version available to your online purchasers. That way the purchaser gets the instant gratification of having the book immediately, while still having the print book turn up a few days later.

Amazon allows you to make the Kindle version of your book available for free or a very low price if the reader purchases the printed version too.

Paper Printing Options

If you are printing your book, then you'll need to decide between Print on Demand (POD), Digital or Offset printing.

Offset printing is the traditional print method used for many years, where the file is transposed into plates, where each of the four colours to be printed (magenta, cyan, yellow, and black) are separated and printed separately, and then overlaid on each other to get the highest density of colour and quality. The pages are laid up usually in 12 or 16 per flat sheet, run through the printers very quickly, and then collated, cut to size using pre-set crop marks set by the designer, and finally the book is bound.

If you are printing more than 1,000 copies of a book, this is usually considered the most cost efficient and highest quality option.

For fewer than 1,000 copies – or, in some cases it's worth considering at 500 – your next best option is to digitally print the book. Using machines that are like very sophisticated photocopiers means the book can be printed straight from the computer file, on individual sheets, then collated, trimmed and bound. These are suitable for as few as one book at a time or many, because the sheets are usually fed into the machine as A4 or A3 size.

As digital printing presses become increasingly sophisticated, the covers and laminating can also be done easily, and the quality is sometimes very hard to distinguish from offset to the untrained eye. However, the drawbacks are still a quality inferior to that gained by offset – especially for colour printing – and a higher cost per book than offset printing in larger quantities.

Having said that, the quality of POD books coming from companies like Amazon and Ingram Spark is excellent with very very user-friendly systems for authors to use.

POD is about printing the book – even in as small a quantity as one at a time – when someone asks for it. The printing cost per book

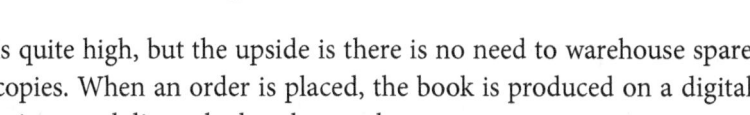

PRINTING OPTIONS

is quite high, but the upside is there is no need to warehouse spare copies. When an order is placed, the book is produced on a digital printer and dispatched to the purchaser.

When seeking a quote from a printer, be sure to specify whether you wish to have offset or digital printing; many printers will offer both, but just as many specialize in one or the other.

Ingram Spark is now changing the status quo for print on demand even more, with their release of the service that enables you to have your book listed on your own website for sales, the order goes directly to Ingram Spark for printing, and the book is delivered directly to the person (reader) ordering it. This has been tested in the USA for the last couple of years and now in 2025 is being made available for authors in other global regions.

This means you as an author can sell directly to your market, without having to go through packing and posting yourself, or selling your book as a PDF online for downloading. Ingram Spark also offer Large Print and Hardcover (with or without jackets) options as well as a range of quality trade paperbacks and paper weights.

If you would like more information or help with uploading to Amazon or Ingram Spark, please take a look at some of the resources on the IndieExperts Publishing website – links at the back of this book. We've even created videos to show you how to do some things and offer training for authors when needed.

Size

You can print in any size at all, but there are economies of scale to be considered with some sizes. For example, if you are offset printing, there may be additional wastage by printing in 'odd' sizes, or with shaped paper (i.e., a round or hexagonal book), which would require a die-cut mold.

Number of Pages

If you are printing in offset, then remember the sheets to be fed will be laid up as 12 or 16 pages per sheet of paper. It is best, therefore, to ensure the number of pages in your book ends up divisible by 12 or 8. It's best to have your designer discuss the printing specifications with your printer to avoid additional wastage or ending up with lots of blank pages at the end of your book.

Paper Stock

Most printers will encourage you to see paper samples before deciding on one you like. If you are new to this, it will pay to remember that most inside pages will be printed on 95–110 gm weighted stock, and most paperback covers for offset will be 250–350 gm weighted stock, and most digital printers will offer 180–250 weight stock for covers. Don't let a printer sell you very expensive, heavier paper for printing unless you intend your book to be a very beautiful coffee table or gift book for which heavier paper is justified. You can easily overspend on this part of your project if you are unfamiliar with paper weights and qualities, and we recommend finding someone to help you with this if you are unsure about your printing quote details.

Colours

You will be asked to specify if your text or the insides in general are black and white, or any other colours. You may wish to print the entire book in navy blue or dark red rather than black ink – but you will need to specify this as 'one colour – navy blue', if so. Otherwise, if the entire insides are simply printed black, then you can ask for 'one colour b/w'.

If you have colour images or text throughout your book, your entire book will need to be treated as a *full- colour* print job – which is a lot more expensive than *one* colour. However, if you only have 2–4 colour images, or the photos are all in the same place, (i.e., in the middle or split evenly in some other way), then these would be printed separately from the rest of the book and collated after printing and before binding.

You MUST discuss your book with your printer before quoting it, so that they know exactly what is required.

Seek recommendations for printers from other authors or industry contacts to find a printer who is used to dealing with books formatted like yours. And we recommend seeking no more than three quotes, as printers in most areas (either geographically or industry specific) talk to each other. If you attempt to get a *lot* of quotes for comparison – if there's a quote going 'right around town' – you'll not gain anything more than annoyed printers. You'll also likely find yourself confused by different jargon and quote layouts too.

Laminating

Even if you want your book to be a matte finish, you'll need to ask for it to be laminated, so that the cover lasts longer than the first time the book is read. Nothing gives away the fact a book has been self-published and cheaply produced than a cover that is not only badly designed but too thin – one that curls, frays at the edges and gets finger marks all over it. Laminating your cover protects it and gives it a much better finish visually.

Some digital printers do not offer this, but it is well worth insisting on.

Binding

The most common types of binding are saddle-stitched, which is stapled through the centre, and is only really suitable for booklets. There is also a saddle-stitched-and-bound option, where the sections of the book that have been offset printed are collected together and stitched (with a thread usually) and then bound together using a glue binding these sections to the spine. This is the most robust option for books, but also the most expensive and not offered by all printers.

The other option is perfect bound – where the pages are all flat set (guillotined) and glued into the book spine. This is the most common, and you are likely to be offered this option for your book. However, there are varying degrees of quality in this option. A good perfect-bound book will stand the test of time (and many repeat readings), and in most cases of short-run books that are not above 300 pages, this is perfectly adequate. If you are unsure about which type of binding best suits your book, discuss it with your printer.

A Word on Kindle E-Books

The way you will need to prepare your Kindle e-book for upload varies slightly from the printed book upload options. For one thing, an e-book is not allowed to have any blank pages, but you are not as restricted by specific dimensions as you are with a printed version. You are also able to easily edit the content of your e-book after it's published, whereas it's much more troublesome to do this with your printed version.

You can also upload your e-book directly from Microsoft Word; in fact, as at the time of updating this book, that's still a good option, unless you have a lot of images and graphics in your book. Kindle also offers its own internal design program that is easy to use.

Because your printed version is going to be far more carefully typeset than your Kindle version, it is best to separate the book files into two separate ones after the final editing phase and before the final typesetting phase. Treat them as two different books in terms of proofing and layout from that point. You can, of course, give them the same cover and all the other parts of the pre-press process are the same, apart from the ISBN number and barcode.

PRINTING OPTIONS

However, back cover text is not required for the e-book but should be used as the *book description* when uploading it.

Once your book is published, you can also send it to editors of other publications for review, but you don't always have to wait for that, and pre-printing advance copies specifically for review is an option to consider.

When your book is *completely finished* and looks the way it's meant to, and you have some quality reviews and feedback from peers, then it's time to do a final proofing – this time for grammar and punctuation. This is a last sweep through by someone who knows how to proof at a very high-quality level. This person will most likely not be the same person you used for the content editing, but a 'fine-tooth comb' detail person who's great with a red pen but knows not to try to re-write the contents. They will also pick up on things like whether references have all been checked, that the index numbers are correct, and that any odd things in the layout are identified.

While one proofer will take responsibility for this, there may be others at this stage who also check the book to ensure that everything is double, and triple, checked.

However, please bear in mind that the chances of your book being 100% error free and totally faultless are never guaranteed. I've known books to have been checked and rechecked up to 20 times and still a reader has come back to the publisher or author and commented on tiny, troublesome things like a double 'and', a comma out of place, or a too-wide gap between some words.

If you accept that your book most likely won't be perfect, but that 98% is a great target to aim for, then your book is likely to get to market sooner and will give you less stress in the final stages of birthing it. However, that is not to say that you should accept anything less than a commitment to the highest possible quality for your book. Obvious and plentiful mistakes that will have your readers running back to you in droves to point out faults are a very unpleasant thing for any author.

One extra piece of advice I'll offer is to set a deadline and commit to getting your book out by that date. If you keep stretching your deadline, you will be more inclined to keep altering the contents, adding and changing things. In these instances, books can take two years to reach completion when they were, in fact, perfectly ready more than one year beforehand.

Your PRODUCTION Checklist

- ☐ Review content
- ☐ Edit content
- ☐ Finalise and sign off content
- ☐ PRE-PRESS
- ☐ Check references
- ☐ Confirm/find/contract
- ☐ Illustrations/diagrams/photos
- ☐ Arrange Foreword to be written
- ☐ Write Introduction
- ☐ Write Dedication
- ☐ Write Acknowledgements
- ☐ Disclaimer
- ☐ Glossary
- ☐ Index created
- ☐ Index checked
- ☐ Table of Contents checked
- ☐ About Author written
- ☐ Pre-print reviews obtained
- ☐ ISBN ordered
- ☐ Barcode obtained
- ☐ Front cover checked
- ☐ Back cover checked
- ☐ Spine checked
- ☐ Print prices obtained
- ☐ Print files checked and approved
- ☐ Files uploaded to printer
- ☐ Kindle Version created
- ☐ Kindle Version uploaded

PRINTING OPTIONS

Your QUOTING Checklist

- [ ] Size of book – exact dimensions
- [ ] Number of pages
- [ ] Paper stock – insides and cover
- [ ] Colour, B/W or one alternative colour?
- [ ] Hard cover or paperback?
- [ ] Laminated cover – matte or gloss?
- [ ] Binding

The Publishing Industry

It's relevant to mention how the publishing industry works and why you should be using your book as part of your marketing strategy, rather than trying to get sales happening through the retail stores.

The publishing industry has changed a lot over the past 100 years, and even more quickly since the development of the digital publishing age. How books are sold, what returns and margins are standard, and how the book distributors and literary agents work is explained in this chapter.

The book industry has been in a state of flux for a long time now. The bookstore chains are found mostly in malls with high rents, and therefore they need to focus on quick turnover. This means that bestsellers and those books which have strong marketing and public relations strategies behind their launch are going to be a lot more attractive to booksellers than nonfiction books by unknown authors.

The nonfiction genre has some advantages and some disadvantages when it comes to distribution. The biggest disadvantage is what is commonly called a 'long tail'. Simply, it works like this:

A novel, cookbook, or biography of someone well known is likely to have a fairly high immediate return, peaking somewhere within the first six months of its launch. A business book or nonfiction inspirational book is likely to peak at about 12–18 months and sustain a reasonably long duration of steady sales, but in smaller numbers per month. For example, a well promoted business book might be still selling an average of 50-100 copies a month after five years, having peaked at around 15,000 copies (in retail sales) at, say, nine months after release. A popular cookbook might have sold that many in the first six months, and maybe only 1,000 more over the next five years in total. (These numbers are as examples only and actual sales will depend on many things, including location and genre.) For retailers, the faster turnover is more attractive and therefore better focused on. This means that back catalogues of some genres are more reliant on independent book sellers and what you, the author, can sell directly by other means.

The reality is that very few retailers will ever sell books directly for an author, and therefore a distribution service is required if you are serious about trying this option. Unfortunately, very few distribution agencies will handle one-off books by unknown authors.

Why am I making it sound so hard to get your book into general retail distribution? Simply because it *is* hard to do – an exercise in frustration for most authors, and very unrewarding financially.

You must remember your reason for writing your book when it comes time to consider distribution. While it's a nice idea to have your book sold through bookstores, the reality is it's more trouble than it's worth. The returns are very low (usually only 35% of Recommended Retail Price after taking out distribution and booksellers' margins – which might mean it's only pennies per item) and make the whole process of getting a book into stores very unprofitable.

Go back to considering why you decided to write a book in the first place, who your market is and what you want them to know about you, your information, and how it will affect them. Use your book as a giveaway, to open doors and get people wanting your consulting, coaching and speaking services.

Sell your book when you speak at events, or on your website. We'll cover this in more detail in chapter 14.

Self-Publishing Your Book

> *Just because you are **self-publishing** your book does not mean you have to lessen the quality of it. This book is designed to walk you through the many stages of getting the ideas out of your head, and into a book that you can use to market yourself, your business and your wisdom.*

Let's recap some of the most important points that we've covered in the previous chapters:

Use Professional Help

It pays to use professionals, not just your cousin or best friend's younger brother. This is true for a number of things relative to your book, but most important when it comes to editing and design.

Some of these next paragraphs may sound repetitive, but as editing and design are the most complex part of the process, it's worth repeating to ensure your complete understanding.

Editing

As outlined already, editing happens in several stages. The first is when you have finished your manuscript and are basically happy with your contents. Give it to a group of beta readers – friends or colleagues who understand your subject and are good at grammar. This is a very helpful part of the process of finishing the manuscript and getting some relevant feedback. The next step is to give your manuscript to an *experienced book editor*. Regardless of how well you think you write, an editor will pick up on things that neither you nor your sub-editor friend will have noticed that relate to the way the reader – your identified target market – will want to read the book.

It may be that some things need to be referenced or explained more simply. Perhaps you've written things that make complete sense to you (and the friend who read through your manuscript) but need clarifying or simplifying. There are also likely times where you've repeated yourself. A good book editor is charged with the task of grooming your raw file and turning it into a reader-friendly book, with chapters that flow, descriptive text that is just right, and no confusing bits.

A book editor will also correct grammar and pick up on spelling mistakes, but a final proofing will still be needed. Some book editors are great with the big picture concept of a book, and some are great at the details. Very occasionally, you'll get one editor who is great at both, but I always recommend using a great content editor and then a separate proofing editor at the end. Fresh eyes always work best when it comes to books.

Also, it's good to use a book editor who is experienced with your genre of book. A nonfiction self-help book will be treated differently from a recipe book (more bullet points and lists) or a novel (more dialogue).

Typesetting, Design, and Offset Printing

The other important step in the process is to use a good designer who understands the intricacies of typesetting and designing a book, not just a magazine, brochure or website.

The following is specifically about printing your book using an Offset Print process. This is what happens at the printers. If you are using Print on Demand (digital printing) then some of these points will not apply.

A book's insides need to have a certain number of pages to fit the printer's requirements and specifications. For example, a book is usually printed on a set number of pages which, when laid up on the machine that prints them, are in multiples of (usually) 16 pages or multiples of eight. So, a book that is 144 pages is laid up in multiples of 16 x 9 pages, but if it's 140 pages, then it's better to re-format it to 136, and lay up in 16 x 8 pages, otherwise you'll end up with four pages blank at the end of your book. A typesetter who is used to these challenges will often come up with options to make this part easy for you.

Another thing that can challenge a new author who is unfamiliar with the pre-press part of the process is that by writing your book in a program like Microsoft Word, you are unlikely to end up with something suitable for offset printing. This is because even though you can convert a finished Word file to a PDF file – which the printers use – the crop marks and various other fine tuning is best turned out from using a program like InDesign or Quark.

If the printers prefer using files that have been created properly from their point of view, then the result is a much better looking book.

If you are only going to print your book as a digitally printed short run – best suited to under 500 copies at a time – then the file produced in Word and then turned into a PDF is not quite so important an issue, because the file is effectively loaded into a giant computer and just printed.

However, an offset printed version of your book – anything over 1,000 copies at a time – is treated differently at the printing stage, with your file output creating plates, which are loaded onto an offset machine that prints large multi-sheet or rolls of paper by running it through ink.

The quality of offset printed books is often much better, and the covers are thicker, so they last longer. However, some books are very well suited to the print on demand option of digitally printing only a few at a time.

A great graphic designer does not necessarily create a great book cover or understand the technical issues of layout for the insides of a book either. They can learn these, of course, but don't make the giant mistake of letting your designer friend learn about book pre-press on your book. There's too much at stake.

You might like to engage the services of a book shepherd or publishing coach to help you work through the many options, especially if this is your first book. They will have experienced the publishing process of many books and be able to help you decide on everything from how to print, what sort of book to produce, how to sell it, and what recommended retail price you may charge for it if you are planning to sell copies.

Book shepherds also usually have access to experienced designers and editors, as well as knowledge about distribution and printing options. This can help you avoid some very expensive learning curves.

Your relationship with a book shepherd or publishing coach is important if you've not published before, as they will guide you through the process, with all the traps and considerations well managed before they become a problem. Most first- or even second-time authors don't know what they don't know yet. Reading this book will help a lot, but there is still much to learn.

Publicity

Google Books

Google Books is an international directory set up by Google to enable books to be located. Their sales details and reviews are visible online – with links through to retail outlets – and the first few pages are readable online. This system enables readers to not only see what the book looks like, but also to read some of the content (without being able to copy or print anything of what they can see on the screen).

To upload a book to Google, you must have a Google mail account and then sign up for approval to Google Books. The upload process is relatively straightforward, and you can either submit the finished book for scanning into their system or a PDF, with separate front and back cover pages.

The great thing about Google Books is that you can specify where the book may be purchased, and link directly to those places. If your book is found mostly on your own website, then people are easily directed there to buy it. If you are unable or unwilling to have it available on Amazon.com, then you can still share with people the relevant information you would otherwise have visible, like the reviews, and a peek inside the pages.

Ingram Spark

Ingram Spark is an excellent print on demand and distribution operating globally. When you upload your book there, you can enable it for Expanded Distribution which then means it's available to be searched and located, then ordered for immediate delivery by 40,000 retail stores, libraries and online book sellers.

Ingram Spark also have catalogues, newsletters that are genre specific and sales data lists that you can have your book listed in for a relatively small fee.

Press Releases

A press release will inform the media about your book when it's available through your distribution system. Even when your book is not available through retail outlets, a press release will help ensure your market finds out about it.

You might also want to send your press release out to podcasters, bloggers, trade organisations, local business networks, clients, and anyone who might be interested in knowing about you and your book. Just because it's called a media or press release, does not mean you can only send it to them.

When you have great news to share, don't advertise it by paying someone to write an 'advertorial'. Instead write a powerful, interesting and attention-grabbing press release aimed at getting editors and program producers to pick up the phone and want more information. Maybe they will interview you, write a feature, or just reprint what you've sent them, but if they think their readers, listeners or viewers will be interested too, you've got an excellent chance of scooping space in their publication or on their station *free*.

When writing a press release:

- **Make the story interesting** – not just self-serving publicity. Use a generic angle; don't just talk about how great *you* are. Talk about the event, situation, opportunity, product. Be clear, succinct, and don't forget to make it sound BIG. Even if you think you are bragging, do it! If you are the only person who's done or doing something, don't hide under a bushel. Step firmly into the spotlight, but explain *why* it's of interest to the audience or readers.

- If you are shy about giving yourself a rave, then ask someone else to write the release for you and give them all the *big* details.

- **Make yourself available for interviews** – put clear contact details at the bottom of the release and invite the recipient of the release to get back to you for more information and/or interview, or in the case of a book release, offer to send a review copy and/or excerpts for publication.

- **Mention who you are** – introduce yourself to the editor or producer with a brief background or bio. Only celebrities who are well-known household names don't have to do this every time a press release is sent out.

- **Don't feel you have to send the release to every media outlet** – select only those who might be particularly interested in your news. The media are overloaded with press releases every day and will block you if you abuse the ability to send your release via online subscriber channels. Be selective!

- **Try to keep to only one page** – this is a teaser for the recipient. Don't 'serve the whole dish' – promote the best and juiciest bits, and you have a better chance of them coming back for more of the whole story if they are interested.

- **Be selective about timing** – don't send it too early or too late.

Yesterday's news is no longer interesting to anyone, but you and tomorrow's news might not even happen.

Identify media to send your press release to:

Media Selection:	Where:
Electronic Media - ☐ Radio ☐ TV ☐ Online Publications	
Print Media - ☐ Magazine ☐ Newspapers ☐ Community publications	
Social Media - ☐ LinkedIn ☐ Facebook ☐ X (formerly Twitter) ☐ Instagram ☐ Pinterest ☐ Online community groups *(Remember to put hyperlinks into your release where appropriate.)*	
Associations and trade connections - Your clients and your own database	

PUBLICITY

> **TIP**
> Try to avoid sending your press releases out to electronic media such as radio, TV, and newspapers when there is a lot of other news happening. For example, if a major earthquake has happened, a war is threatening, or a political issue is hotly brewing, reporters and editors tend to be more focused on bigger and more urgent news. While you can't always plan around this, sometimes you can delay a release until whatever is currently on page one is a little more settled.

Check the following:

- Your press release has a powerful, attention-grabbing headline.
- Don't make it 'all about you' in a self- promotional way but keep the end audience/readers in mind. What interests them? Keep it generic – the release is a teaser which you hope editors/producers will be interested enough in to follow up and interview you for more information.
- Put a clear set of contact information at the end so that editors/producers can contact you and follow up for more information.
- *Proofread and double-check the quality of the writing* – remember you are sending this to professional communicators who will not bother to read anything that's unprofessionally presented.
- Finally, check it again – if you were reading this story in a magazine or newspaper, would you think it was *interesting*, or *just self- serving rubbish?*

IDEA TO AUTHOR-ITY

Press Release - 11 January 2025
International Recognition for Local Inventor
<Bold headline>

Local businessman turned inventor John Jones has been awarded a prestigious contract to supply ....

This is where you write the real story – what's happened, who does it involve, why is it of interest to the editor who will read this – and make it sound compelling and NOW.

Next paragraph is where you put some background to the story or situation.

Summarize the story a little more.

John Jones has been... <*write a 100–150-word outline here and have it proofed before sending*>

For more information, please contact John Jones at: <Email>, or <Phone>

Now let's review this as though John Jones wrote a book:

Ready to Get the Word Out?

You wrote the book—now let's make sure people *find it and read it*. With smart strategy and promotion that actually works, **Indie Experts Publishing** has your back.

Let's help you shine: *www.indieexpertspublishing.com*

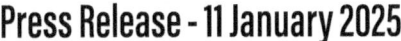

PUBLICITY

Press Release - 11 January 2025

Local Inventor Shares Trade Secrets to Sports Industry Marketing <Bold headline>

Multi award-winning businessman turned inventor John Jones has been encouraged to share the secrets to his success in commercialising supply chain opportunities for the international sports industry. ....

This is where you write the real story – what's happened, who does it involve, why is it of interest to the editor who will read this – and make it sound compelling and NOW.

His book – Sports Savvy Supply Chains – is a comprehensive look at how anyone struggling to get their big ideas into sports industry supply chains can hack simple but lesser known tendering processes ...

Next paragraph is where you put some background to the story or situation.

Jones has been a classic rags to riches story having gone from selling Rugby Socks out of his garage to pioneering the bamboo sports kits featured by nearly every Football club in the deep south since 1999.

Summarize the story a little more.

John Jones has been... <write a 100–150-word outline here and have it proofed before sending>

His tales of knocking on doors and being willing to get a little crazy in challenging an outdated customer service culture is compelling reading, and his book is sure to enlighten those who get caught up in tendering regulations.

To review a sample copy, to invite John Jones to be interviewed, or to learn more about this book, please visit www.johnjones.com/media

When you send a press release out you want to ensure that the recipient can go directly to a pre-prepared website landing page that gives the right information about the book and you the author.

A Media Page, is one of the website pages you need to set up, these three being:

About The Book: A sales page with cover, sample chapter, links to the many places where a reader can purchase the book. If that's also on your website, then ensure that the purchasing options are clear, easy to navigate and all links are working.

Call to Action: This is only available via the links in the back section of your book. This is where to go if your readers want more information, to access the resources or bonus material mentioned in the book, or to learn more about a specific program or service. They can trade their email address for the promised bonus material and you can then follow up with them over time with more offers, bonus material, next book information, and reminders to please leave a review.

The Media Page: this is where you have the high-res versions of a downloadable cover page of your book, some relevant information about your ability to be interviewed for podcasts, radio or news channels, and an invitation to get in touch to arrange a speaking/interview opportunity.

These three website pages are what you need to have in place when your book launches to ensure that readers can take action in the appropriate way you wish them to when they want to know about your book, and your services.

Distribution

Even before you have had your books printed and they are ready to launch into the world, you must address the issue of where you are going to sell them, who you will sell them to, and how they can obtain copies.

Printed Books

The way the distribution industry for books works has always been based *mostly* on this system:

The author works through a publisher, the publisher works through a distribution agent, and the distribution agent sells the books to the bookstores and libraries. It used to be that authors could sell their books directly to bookstores (in very rare cases this still happens, but usually only when the independent bookstore is known personally to the author). Publishers could also once sell directly to stores and libraries, but with the number of books now being produced in all markets, nearly all booksellers insist on working with distribution agents only, and distribution agents work only with authors and publishers with at least a dozen titles.

The reason for these changes is simplification of administration. As margins are increasingly squeezed in retail, and by publishers, everyone is trying to be more efficient, and so the process has become more streamlined with fewer individual players, but it does mean extra intermediaries, and therefore extra complications for authors.

The outcome is that unless you have more than a good handful of titles to offer, you are hampered by having to work through other people to sell your books on your behalf, to try to get them into stores and therefore available to your readers.

The margins are also very tight and make this quite uneconomic.

For example:

The book might have a RRP of $30.00 including sales tax of 10%. (However, in some countries like New Zealand the GST is 15%).

- **$ 30.00 RRP**
- - $3.00   Tax 10%
- - $12.15   Retailer's margin 45% of $27.00
- **$14.85**   Wholesale Price
- - $2.97   Distributor's commission 20
- **$11.88   Net**
- $6.50   Cost of printing
- $ 5.38   Net return to author. If you are working with a publishing company, this might end up as only $1.18 (10% of the net).

If your books are costing you $4–$8 each, this is a hard way to make any money out of your knowledge.

If you sell direct from your website, then the difference between what you make out of your $20–$30 book, and what it costs you to print, is considerably better; you could even throw in free post and packaging and your return will still be well ahead of the retail trade option.

DISTRIBUTION

One thing not widely publicized in the book sales industry is the issue of Returns. This is where if the book store purchases copies from the publisher or distribution company working for the publisher, and those books do not sell, then after a certain period of time (and in some cases this can be up to 12 months) those books are returned to the publisher.

The cost of returns is usually passed on to the author, and you could easily end up having to repay much of what you earned in initial sales. There are reporting methods used around the world that don't seem to reflect the true value of the sales vs returns on an industry level, but it is estimated that as many as 25% of books are returned on a regular basis.

When listing your book on Ingram Spark, you have the option to select 'no' to returns if your books are purchased by book sellers. Because this is a widely accepted practice now, most book sellers will only sell books they are specifically asked for via this print on demand method. This is another good reason to not rely on selling your books via retail stores as a primary means of distributing them.

Getting Your Book onto Amazon

One of the first things that people want to know about publishing is how to get their books onto Amazon.

Amazon is a great place to sell your books if you have an international market. However, check the fine print carefully if you are outside the USA, Canada, and the UK. To get paid, you'll need to have a USA tax code, which means filling in a series of forms and extra paperwork to ensure you have all your tax agreements in place. This may sound easy, but I assure you it can take a lot of mucking around if you are not used to tax rules in your own country or the USA. Amazon does provide a lot of information about this on their website but be prepared to read a lot of fine print and for it to take time to sort out.

This also affects Kindle – which is owned by Amazon.com.

You used to need to have a distribution system set up in the USA or Canada or the UK if you wished to sell printed books via Amazon.com – because they need to know that if sales are happening, they can get stock immediately (not from thousands of miles away) to fulfil their order obligations.

Using the POD option provided by Amazon or Ingram Spark offers a great alternative to this, but there are some cost issues to consider.

Amazon's Royalty Calculator

There are several ways to work out the returns on your book sales, and one of the best tools to use is www.Shinywords.com/tools/royalty-calculator

Here's a simple example:

Amazon KDP Royalty Calculator

BookBird's Sales Calculator estimates daily and monthly book sales based on the Amazon Best Sellers Rank (BSR). This allows you to discover profitable books and niches with just a few clicks.

Book Format: Paperback

Interior Type: Black & White

Marketplace: Amazon.com

Page count: 100

List Price ($): 15

Cost Breakdown

List price	$ 15.00
Minimum List Price	$ 5.37
Printing Cost	$ 2.15
Amazon Fee	$ 6.00

Calculated Royalties

Standard Royalty	$ 6.85
Extended Distribution	$ 3.85

You can see that you'll make $6.85 per book in royalties for each book you sell on their standard plan. Amazon takes $8.15 per book including the cost of manufacturing it.

Take out withholding tax – if you set up your accounts properly this should only be 5%. Payments are made only when there is more than $100 in your account.

If you have a marketing strategy that includes directing people to Amazon.com, then this might be worth exploring and signing up for, but if you don't, then your book might just as easily sell a few dozen a year, and your royalties will be nothing to celebrate.

The Three Rs

However, remember that there are three great reasons to use Amazon as a key distribution point for your book:

1. **Real Estate:** There is a lot of space in the Amazon store for every book listed. You can use this space FREE, to list your book, use a great description, employ good keywords, extra information about you as the author, and additional marketing information using the A+ Content feature. All of this is FREE marketing space where people are buying books.

2. **Rankings:** When a book first lists, and any time you promote it after that, your book will be ranked according to it's popularity. It pays to promote it – especially in the first few weeks – so that your rankings can be seen and even celebrated if you reach a #1 status. This will help your market to feel encouraged to buy your book.

3. **Reviews:** In any form of marketing, social proof is important. Having people give your book 4 or 5 stars is a great way to ensure that others who see your book doing well, and can read comments left for your book, will feel inspired to read it.

If you are using your book as a marketing tool, then this will be something that means a lot to people checking you out. If someone wants to book you to speak about your topic, then ensuring that they can see your success as an author might also help increase your fees and credibility for engagements to speak or deliver workshops.

Other places you can sell to or through:

Association or franchises linked to your topic. Invite them to promote your book to their members, or better, to buy enough to give away to all members as a special promotion.

Your clients. Those you know who will benefit and might also share details of a special offer to their clients. For example, if your book is about accounting for small businesses, ask a selected group of accountants to review the book, and then offer a special deal for them to offer to their clients – this could add up to hundreds of books per accountant – which makes them look good to their clients, and you have an easier sales process than approaching individual companies.

Marketing to your entire database. Include in this group your online social media contacts to get them interested in buying your book directly.

Selling your book at the back of the room. When you speak at training or conference events as the guest speaker on your specialist topic.

Give the book away to delegates. Anyone attending a convention you are presenting at and working the cost of one book per person into your speaker fees.

Talk it up: From Pages to Stages

Now that you have a book, you can use it as a marketing tool and door-opener to the organisations you most want to speak at, train for, or consult to. Here are a few things you can do to maximise the opportunities ahead.

Send a copy with a cover letter to the person who books speakers/trainers in the organisations you have already determined are a good fit for your expertise. Tell them that you are available for a meeting to discuss their needs and to determine if there is any potential for you to do some business together in the future. Make this all about *them*, not just a rave about you or your book. However, be sure to reference the fact that your book is new, and that you've sent a signed copy for their personal library.

Cite a reference to and bookmark any particular chapter that you feel they might find most interesting in relation to their current business or industry issues (making it clear you've done your homework already) and that you are seeking further opportunities to meet if/when the time is suitable to do so.

Follow up with them a week later to ensure they have received your book and letter. There's a good chance that they will at least have checked the chapter you bookmarked. By then, they may be willing to agree to a meeting or at least give you a few minutes on the phone answering any pre-prepared questions you may have about their conference plans or training opportunities.

You can offer to send them more information if they agree to receive it. At the very least, ask if you can keep in touch by calling again in a few months. This keeps the door open even if they are not willing or able to see you right away. Your book can be the wedge that potentially keeps the door ajar.

Speaking

Do you want to be a trainer? Do you like the interaction of workshops and small group seminars, or are you hungry for the big stages and love keynote presentations best? One of the things you need to determine as you go through your journey from **Idea to Author-ity**® is the best way to work to your strengths as a professional expert.

Back-of-the-Room Sales

Selling from the back of the room (BOR) takes skill and preparation.

Don't try to be selling books after your presentation yourself, when this time is best used to connect directly with people who want to give you their cards or ask you questions. Get someone else to do this part for you but make it very easy for them. Don't overcomplicate your systems for payments or bundling of products.

Have a clear price point for each item you are selling (if more than just one or two books) and give your audience a compelling reason to buy *today* rather than go online to order later. They are far more likely to purchase on the spot than get around to it later.

This compelling reason might take the form of a special price or a bundle of two or more products together for a premium rate on the day.

If you don't have an assistant to help with this, one way to make it easy on yourself and those wishing to buy your books is to create a form on which the purchaser can write their name, phone number, and credit card details (complete with name on card and expiry date, plus signature). Ask that they work on an honesty system.

The chances are you'll get very few people who will be dishonest when doing this, as many speakers who have tried this can attest to. When you consider the cost of your book and the amount you might have to pay an assistant, this is a risk well worth taking.

By asking for a phone number, you can still contact them later to check any details if something is amiss.

Online Marketing Options

You will need to build a good presence online for your book, one that fits with the position you are establishing for yourself as a professional expert. Start by creating a webpage on your existing site just to promote your book before it's ready to launch.

Put extracts and teasers about your book there and use good search engine optimization (SEO) techniques based on quality key words, so that people searching for the topic(s) your book focuses on can start to find you and your book information online.

Turn some of the longer sections of your book into blogs rich with good key words and tagged appropriately for SEO purposes. Then spend a few minutes every day posting snippets, comments and media commentary and opinions (appropriately) on your Facebook and X (Twitter) accounts.

Build up a following of people who want to know what you know and how you can help them, so that when your book is ready to be sold, you can ensure they know about it through that online reputation you are now building using the social media resources available to you.

Now let's look at each of these tasks in more detail.

Create a Web Page

As mentioned in the chapter about Publicity, you will need more than just one web page for your book. It used to be that people would recommend having an entire website for each book you write. I believe you need three landing pages on your current website instead. Start by registering your book's title as a domain name if you can and have that URL pointing to the first landing page on your website – the About the Book page. Talk with your webhost about this to make it easy and straightforward if this is new territory for you.

By registering a new domain name for your book, you can refer people directly to that part of your website without having to worry about extra-long URL descriptions. For example, if your book is titled *ACME Great Ideas*, you can create marketing messages that simply refer to www.acmegreatideas.com, rather than www.mycompany.com/acmegreatideas/book – which sounds a lot longer when you say it out loud.

For as little as $20 per year, you can register your domain name at a variety of hosting sites, and then have your domain name pointing to a particular web page.

About the Book – Sales Page

Display the book title and subtitle prominently on the web page, and make it clear what your book is about if the title is a little ambiguous. In fact, using the title as the URL page title is a very good idea. Search engine marketing experts may recommend using important keywords in the title, but let's keep it simple and focus on ensuring people know the title and subtitle. Then visitors to the site will know they have reached the right page.

Overview of Your Book

Write a quick summary at the top of the page. Cover the key points succinctly and create interest and questions in the mind of your visitor, so that they keep reading and scroll down the page or click through to more information. Remember that this is a sales page.

Who is Your Ideal Audience?

What sort of person is going to want to buy your book? Consider what key issues they may have that you can help them to resolve.

For example:

"Are you struggling with bullies at work?"

"Do you get nervous about presenting in public?"

"Do you want to know how to make more money while you travel?"

"If you have great photography skills, here's how to commercialize your talent."

Choose situations that prospects are already thinking about, so it's easy for them to identify with you. The broader you make these situations, the more likely your site visitor will identify with them. However, don't become so broad you're no longer credible.

Keep it tight. Instead of 'Here's how to be a better leader', talk about 'Here's 10 ways to improve your leadership style when dealing with teenagers.'

Benefits ('What you will learn')

List the benefits they will gain from reading the book.

For example:

"Your team will be more productive and engaged in creating higher-quality widgets."

"You can easily sell your stories to magazines using these simple techniques."

"You'll create more measurable opportunities every day."

The more general your claims, the more your prospects will identify with them. However, again, if you make your claims too broad, you run the risk of being seen as not credible. For example, if you're writing about selling techniques, it's reasonable to promise, 'you'll talk to more prospects', but it's stretching credibility to claim, 'You'll sell double the number of widgets every day.'

Testimonials

Insert one or two strong, benefit-oriented testimonials about the book, as provided by the people who've read a draft copy.

You could also include relevant testimonials about you and your services, but it's best to focus on the book first, and you as the author second. After all, you want to have people buy the book. Once they have done that, they will get a strong feeling about your level of skill, ability, history, etc.

Ensure that your reviewers are also relevant to your topic. It's pointless having a famous wealth coach say great things about your book on raising children when they may not even have children themselves – no matter how many books they've sold on making money.

About the Author

Write a brief one-paragraph biography of you, and why you have the credibility to write this book. You've already written this content in the book's Introduction, so you can extract some of the text from there.

Include a small head-and-shoulders photograph of you at this point on the page.

By the way, even if your website already has an 'About Us' page with your biography and photograph, repeat it here so website visitors get all the information about the book in one place, without having to click elsewhere.

Give away a Sample

Provide a PDF file for downloading. Make it a powerful chapter from the book. You can also use the Amazon Look Inside feature to show not only the book sample chapters on your website but this will also take readers directly to the appropriate Amazon sales page to purchase with one click.

Make them available here as simple PDF links, so site visitors can click to download them immediately. Don't force them to fill in a form before they can download it; make the process as simple as possible.

Bonuses

If you're offering any additional products or services for buyers of the book, list them here. This is an optional section, and you don't have to include it. However, low-cost high-value bonuses can greatly increase the perceived value of their purchase. For example, you could offer:

- The e-book version for immediate download, so they don't have to wait for delivery.
- These following items could be on the sales page, or alternatively on the Call-to-Action page for after they read the book.

- Additional articles on similar topics you've written.
- Downloadable worksheets or templates.
- Password-protected access to videos or other resources on your website.

Orders

Include a link to a secure credit-card ordering process for them to buy the book. If you already have this sort of process available for selling other products on your website, simply do the same for your book. If you don't have any system in place, use PayPal, or Stripe for payments that takes just minutes to set up.

If you are happy to send everyone to your Amazon page, this is easy, as you then don't have to worry about processing sales and sending the books out to customers. Some authors find this a much easier option and there are a couple of benefits to doing this.

If all your online sales are via Amazon, then your rankings as an author and the book's individual rankings are easily listed. This is always relevant when you are thinking global.

When your customers see your book is ranked in the top 100, or 500 in its category on Amazon, potential buyers will see extra value in your book. Also, whenever you are in the top sections, your Amazon promotional algorithms are strengthened, and your book becomes easier to find and identify among those others in your category. People can easily search by topic on Amazon, so your rankings do matter.

Another thing you can do on Amazon is paid promotions where you link your book to others which are popular in your category. For example, you may see where it says, "Other people who viewed this book also viewed ___". This is sponsored marketing for authors.

Articles

Create some short articles and blogs from your content. You don't have to re-write from scratch items you've already had edited and have confidence in for their quality. If it was good enough to use in your book, it's good enough to use as an article and submit to other publications.

Aim for 400–800 words per article, with a focus on high-quality content that readers can take away and use immediately. Don't worry about giving away the best content from your book; just give it away and the people who value it will buy the book anyway.

E-mail Newsletter

Use something like Mail Chimp, which is an opt-in newsletter format you can use on your website for people to sign up to and then receive an online newsletter once a month featuring one of these articles. You can include some self-promotion in the newsletter as well, but most of the newsletter is the feature article.

Don't create a separate newsletter just for the book; that's creating unnecessary additional work. But use the book content to create interest in the book via sending these articles and extracts.

Write a Blog

Once a week, put some of the smaller extracts into a blog.

If you don't have a blog yet, get one! It's one of the most powerful online tools you have for establishing yourself as an author-ity. Unlike your email newsletter, your blog remains permanently on the Internet, just like a website. (In fact, a blog *is* a website.)

Serious Internet marketers use formats like WordPress, a great platform for creating your whole website on that keeps the blog and the website well connected. **There's a bonus article** about how and why WordPress is ideal for authors and speakers at the very end of this e-book.

Podcast

A podcast is an audio newsletter. In principle, it's like an email newsletter, where subscribers opt in to receive messages. They get the messages automatically when you publish them. However, instead of receiving articles in their email inbox, they receive audio clips in their podcast software and on their audio player.

Turn your blog into a podcast by recording it as an audio file, then publish it to your podcast. This is a hugely popular option. It's easy to do, and a large segment of many markets prefer listening to short audio files while walking or driving or working out at the gym.

Because you're simply reading your articles out loud, you don't have to spend extra time finding new material for your podcast.

Create a Video

The next step is to produce a video version of your article (with you speaking to camera), which you publish to YouTube. The way someone talks about something and the way something is read is slightly different, so practise a few times reading through your words. Then relax, and instead of 'reading it through', discuss the information. This makes it sound a lot friendlier and easier for the viewer to enjoy too.

One way to get around the 'I hate talking to the camera' feeling that many people get when they start doing this is to seat yourself slightly side-on to the camera and make the whole piece look like you are talking to an off-camera interviewer.

Video is daunting for some people, and you might find your first few attempts feel and look awkward. But don't give up. Video is such an important online communication tool that it's worth persisting.

Special Reports

So far, we've only looked at techniques for making use of one article at a time. But we're not done yet. We can get even more leverage by combining articles.

Why not take a handful of your articles and combine them into a Special Report? You might title this 'Seven great ways to…' or 'The three most common mistakes to avoid when….'

Write this in Word and add an introduction promoting you and your business. Include your contact details on the cover or a special page at the end. Then save it in PDF format and give it away to as many people as possible.

Host Webinars

Start running regular webinars for your network based on the topics you write about. You may have to invite people to be there FREE, but as you develop a following and develop more products and training materials, you might also consider offering paid programs using this format. At the end of the webinar, you can promote your book and other relevant products and services.

Webinars take some skill and practice, so they are not for everybody. However, if you do take the time to learn the technology and practise presenting them, you'll find they are extremely powerful marketing tools.

Even if you're not a skilled presenter, you can run effective webinars, especially because you don't have to design the presentation from nothing – most of it is already in the articles you've written.

Social Media

Don't overlook the importance of using Facebook, X (Twitter) and You Tube for promoting your book. Set up an account for each of these, ensure your branding and usernames are appropriate to your book, your own name or your company, and include some of your already identified keywords in your descriptions about your site. Also ensure each is linked back to your website, and arrange for your blog to be automatically set up to create a post on your Facebook and X pages.

Every time you write a blog or post an article, your Facebook page and X feed will post a link to it, which, as your followers grow in number, will alert them all to your latest offers.

The key to making your social media sites really work for you is to ensure you always post good, useful content for those who like what you do, your followers. They will even share and repost or re-tweet some of your best information, further helping you to grow your connections.

The overall thing to keep in mind is to be the expert you are, and ensure you are constantly being that person. To the market you want to work with, the 'go to' expert is the one who demonstrates a range of knowledge and expertise, supported by experiences worth sharing with their market. Be visible, be approachable, and share graciously.

Pulling it All Together

The entire journey of 'Idea to Author-ity' has been a personally challenging one due to the changing landscape of publishing over the last 20 years. When I started my company to assist people in writing and publishing their books with the intention of doing a much higher-quality job of it than through the vanity publishing option, I was one of only a handful of publishers working this way. Now many who do this, including many traditional publishing houses – yes, even the really big ones – have developed a division within their company to charge authors for the privilege of helping them to get started as they write and publish their first book. What I've outlined in this book is based on what I've learned through trial, error, experience, and most of all talking with many authors and publishers – of all types and sizes – through the last 23 years. I've attended international book fairs and worked with literary agents, sold foreign rights deals, and secured high-quality traditional publishing contracts for authors. I've also worked with a small handful of authors who are represented by companies who are considered to be the giants of the industry, and while the publishing side of things was an easy option for them, I found the subsequent marketing and distribution was not so well supported after the first few weeks of their book's release.

I'm passionate, therefore, about the entire journey – from having that first idea to becoming an award-winning, highly respected authority in your field of expertise. In order to do that, you need to allow for an incredible commitment of time and energy, to want that as an outcome so much that the frustrations of the journey don't swamp your enthusiasm for it, and to be willing to invest in learning new things – or sometimes, spending money on having someone else do those things for you. Becoming an author is an expensive decision.

But here's how it can all come together to serve you.

Write a *really* good book. Publish it on Amazon and any other platforms that appeal to you. Get good reviews and monitor your author and book rankings. Support this with excellent social media, blogs and newsletters to your existing contacts, and some advertising. The better your ranking and the more books you are selling, the better you are able to put a great press release or article into the hands of the general media or your industry trade publications and respectfully 'demand' (or at least put forth a very good argument for why) they write a good story about you, your book, and what you have to offer your market. This is one time – and you can build on this multiple times – that you can proudly wave your publicity under the noses of the market you most want to work with and capitalize on that to get paid for the expert work you do best.

By writing a book about what you are an expert in or have advanced knowledge or experiences with, you can easily position yourself as being *the* best person in your field to help solve the biggest challenges faced by your potential market. The easiest thing to do is create a book that really gives value and shares much of what you know; in turn, it inspires people who need what you have or know to request more help from you personally.

You may have a whole team of people you work with, or you may work alone. Either way, when you become an author-ity about your subject, your credibility increases in the minds of those who have read your book. Your team will also benefit from increased requests for your services too – by being busier. But personally, your fees

might increase, and so will your chances of speaking to groups about what you do. Your own knowledge about your subject will expand too, as you refine your knowledge even further through researching and writing your book.

If others have also written about your subject, then you will have joined the ranks of those *author-ities* by virtue of having written a book. This won't necessarily mean you are competing more fiercely with them, but perhaps this opens the door to more collaboration with them as you gain a better understanding of the similarities and differences in your individual perspectives on the subject matter.

I hope this has demonstrated just how easy it can be to write, publish and then market a book, one that will clearly articulate to your target market just exactly why they should seek your services – and be prepared to pay a fair and reasonable fee for them (and not a discounted one) – because you are an expert at what you do.

Use your book to open doors, continue to expand your knowledge and expertise, and keep learning how to leverage that too.

Most of all, have fun signing copies of your book, and watch out for the readers in airports and cafes who just happen to be reading a copy of your book. Feel that thrill of knowing you are reaching people well beyond your current networks.

Bonus Chapter

Using WordPress® as Your Website Platform

WordPress Websites for Speakers and Professional Experts

For me as a coach of speakers and authors, and as someone who also has a strong focus on marketing, the subject of websites is a hot one, and I've assisted in several ways to get speakers' websites up and running from thought to completion and then ongoing maintenance. I'm therefore writing this from the perspective of my own experiences and knowledge, but I will clearly state I am not a *technical* WordPress wizard.

This brings me to the first important point I believe needs to be clearly addressed with regard to websites in general.

There are designers and then there are website designers. They are not necessarily the same. Someone who can do great brochures may not also be great at online design. I even know a great website designer who could not design business cards.

Rule #1 for getting a new website designed: Hire a good website designer.

Another good thing to know is that many designers are terrible copy writers – and vice versa, of course. Your designer may not be a good choice of writer, or even project manager, for the development of your website.

Rule #2: Consider the people on the team required for the development of a new website.

A great website will most likely have been developed by a team, not just a web designer. Your team should consist of people with the following skills:

- Design skills
- Technical, including coding
- Copywriting
- SEO specialist
- Social media expertise

And maybe a project manager to ensure everything gets done and all parties pull together to produce the best result.

This brings me to the subject of WordPress as a platform for websites, especially for professional speakers and service providers.

Platforms for Building Websites

Your website needs to be created with something. Options include programs such as Jumla, very comprehensive sites might use Magenta, or your website creator might be using their own hard coding program which is sometimes hard to use by others. This problem has been known to frustrate people everywhere if you try to change hosts or take over more control of the site. Many different platforms are used, and one of the biggest frustrations with websites is that as we become more technically savvy, we collectively seem to want to take over more direct control of our sites rather than relying on (and paying for) web-geeks to make all the required updates and changes for us.

Along comes WordPress, and it's a total game-changer. Suddenly, this exceptionally easy-to-use platform is putting the control back in everyone's own hands, and the cost of creating and therefore maintaining our websites is dramatically reduced.

WordPress started out as a free blog site and in a remarkably short number of years has become the preferred choice of more than 100 million website owners as a free-ware platform.

According to statistics managed by ManageWP, WordPress sites get more unique visitors per day than Amazon. According to Wikipedia, one quarter of the world's websites are hosted on a WordPress platform.

It took a very short time for even hard-core designers to start loving the exceptional functionality and easy use that WordPress offered, and the level of power it put into the hands of their clients.

As far as design goes, there are hundreds of design themes. More than 40,000 plugins mean there are virtually *endless* options for making your site look and function the way you want it to.

So where does that leave the designers?

While pretty well anyone can log on, start up and create something, using a website designer who is also a WordPress wizard is a great idea because you may still need some hard coding and 'tricky bits' worked out to ensure your site is *exactly* what you want it to be. And working with someone like that also helps the stress levels when or if you happen to need technical help with your site any time in the future.

I've been working on my own and my clients' WordPress sites for nearly 18 years, and while I'm very proficient at lots of aspects of the program, I rely heavily on a couple of technical experts I can call on any time to ensure all is okay if I'm poking around in the engine room.

Using different themes and APPs, you can specify the colours, banner design elements, number of columns, and shape and layout of the site you want, and then your designer can set that up for you. That is where the next exciting part of the development starts.

As I mentioned before, your designer may not be the same person as your copy writer or your project manager. In some companies, these teams work together with a client; in other situations, the three or four people involved may be external colleagues from different companies who contract into the same projects together. Sometimes it's only two people if the copy writing, design, and project management of the development phase is shared between the designer and the writer.

The way I work with clients on these is to engage a highly competent website designer who has a general design background, and then I project manage the development and do the copy writing and extra set-up parts beyond the actual design and technical set-up. I also have another website-only designer who is great at the high-tech, SEO, and basic design parts of a site.

Back to the 'exciting' stage of the development…

With WordPress, someone who has reasonable technical skills and who is a good writer or project manager can take over the balance of the set-up of the site once the technical and basic design is completed. That's how easy and flexible a WordPress platform can be.

For professional speakers and service providers, this means that you can easily learn how to manage and update your own site. There are some aspects of the back end or 'engine room' best avoided by newbies, but there's not a lot you can't do once you get the hang of it. And that's one of the main reasons why it's such a popular platform.

Another reason is that so much functionality is available on a WordPress site. Plugins are available – optional extras like opt-in sign ups, event tabs, shopping carts, and many more. Many of the plugins and themes are free too. With WordPress, your site won't get left behind and need to be renewed for technical reasons, even though a refreshed design will often be a good idea every few years. You can still update with what you have rather than completely starting from scratch each time you update.

Rule #3: Decide how you want your site to look at the start in terms of what theme you wish to use.

Having some idea of whether you want a column on one side or two, a boxy look, or maybe no columns at all is part of the early development. Changing themes is not straightforward once your site is live; in fact, that should be treated as a 'new design' mission.

Domain Names and Building Your Site

Setting up your site on a domain name 'www.mysite.com' involves ensuring your site is created on a live site, even though the site itself won't be seen by anyone until it's released. Let me explain. Your domain name is the name of your website, and a WordPress site is created on a platform which is effectively 'live on a domain name', and therefore you will have already worked out your hosting options ahead of the site being built.

The site can then be built up and made ready for the world to see in a totally hidden way – perhaps with a landing page associated with that domain name which is a fancy 'under construction' page until you take that curtain page away when you are ready to release your site.

Once the site is ready to come out from behind the curtain, you may find things you wish to tweak, change, and add, but don't let perfection hold you back. Your site may continue to evolve for years. It's not always a matter of having to 'build a new website' next time you get inspired to make some changes on your site. You can simply use the ever-evolving opportunities with WordPress to grow your site through the years.

One more point about domain names: if you have paid for them, you own them. Where they are hosted is entirely over to you. Your website host does not own your domain name (unless you have asked them to register that for you and never paid them for it). You own it, and you have complete control of when and where you might want to change its parking garage.

You should expect to pay around $20–$30 per month for hosting. You might be looking at anything from $500–$2,500 for design and copywriting. And for a project manager service allow a little more. Essentially, you can have a website that recently might have meant an investment of $10,000–$20,000 for as little as $4,000–10,000.

When you start to consider a new website using WordPress as a platform, expect this to be a 'how long is a piece of string' matter when it comes to cost. It depends on how much input you need from your designer, copy writer, and project manager.

If you are a professional speaker, using a project manager might be a good idea if they know their way around a WordPress back end and can help bring out the really important information and present it effectively.

Rule #4: Your site can look and function any way you want it to. WordPress is totally flexible.

Search Engine Optimization

SEO is incredibly easy on WordPress because the search engines love WordPress. WordPress also has exceptionally easy SEO plugins that make optimizing the site and every page a two-minute job.

If you are writing a blog – and you should be – one on WordPress is arguably much better ranked and found on Google than any other option for blogging. And the best part of using WordPress for your blog is that it can be all done on the same site – you don't need a separate blog site for your blog. It's all tied together seamlessly.

Disclaimer: This bonus chapter is based on all the things I frequently find myself explaining to my clients about using WordPress and why I and others feel that WordPress is a great option for authors and professional speakers to use for their websites. I am not a certified WordPress expert, designer, or website guru by any other name; however, I am frequently involved with people who are, and so have a much better than average understanding of WordPress. If I've misstated any information above, please feel free to leave a comment and correct me.

About Dixie Maria Carlton

A successful author, publisher, international speaker and coach, Dixie has taken hundreds of authors, industry experts and business specialists **from Idea to Author-ity®**.

As a well-travelled digital nomad, Dixie has worked with clients from a variety of industries all over the world. Dixie's special skills in marketing, brand development, publishing, speaking and coaching make up her essential toolbox when working with highly motivated entrepreneurs who want to change their corner of the world.

Dixie's mission is to help bring their important messages that matter to their target market. By Educating and Empowering authors to understand the landscape of the journey from Pages to Stages. She is exceptional at strategy, able to clearly see the big picture and understand the details. She is described by clients as methodical, knowledgeable and inspirational.

To request more information on how you can work with Dixie, or have her speak at your next event, please email:

Dixie@dixiecarlton.com

You can access Dixie Maria Carlton's Author Page via this link:

www.tinyurl.com/DMCarlton

www.dixiecarlton.com

Facebook.com/dixiecarltonauthor

Twitter.com/dixiecarlton

Instagram.com/dixiethewordwitch

From Idea to Authority— This Is Just the Beginning

Whether you're still shaping your big idea, halfway through writing, or already holding your book in hand—you don't have to figure it all out alone.

At **Indie Experts Publishing**, we've helped hundreds of non-fiction authors go from mapping out their message to marketing their finished book with confidence. Wherever you are on the journey, we're here to guide your next step— and then, the one after that.

Ready to turn your knowledge into influence?

Take our Readiness to Publish Quiz and find out where you're at on the path:
www.indieexpertspublishing.com/authority-authors

Up Next in the Authority Author Series

Authority Island

A simple tale of three authors, three ways to write and publish a book, three different outcomes....

Read an excerpt here

What nonfiction authors really need to know about getting leverage on their authority.

Whether you're writing nonfiction e-books or selling your expertise as a writer of blogs and articles, the business of being a writer is exactly that: a business. It's a business for authors and experts who speak, retired professionals, people who have something to say and maybe want to change their corner of the world in some way. But once the book is written, then the hard work begins as you tackle the difference between being an author vs an authority.

This book covers areas authors need to know including **file uploading, publishing options, social media, media training, planning your book and speaking professionally about your topic.** These things may be unfamiliar to many authors at the start of their writing and publishing journey but are critical to the success of any book.

Authority Island is a fictional tale describing the respective experiences of three nonfiction authors.

Other Books by Dixie Maria Carlton

Nonfiction
- Start with a Draft
- Authority Island
- The Taboo Conversations/That Sex Book
- Advertising, Branding & Marketing 101
- Golden Nuggets: Wise Ideas for Young People Who Grow up and Go

Collaborative books featuring Maria Carlton
- The Power of Promotional Products
- The Power of More Than One
- The Power of More Than One – v2
- 20/20 – A Fresh Look at Business Growth
- 20/20 – A Fresh Look at Inspiration
- Create the Business Breakthrough You Want

Dixie also writes fiction as Dixie Carlton
- A Song Out of Time – Part 1 of the Margaret McKenzie Story
- Rhythm and Rhyme – Part 2 of the Margaret McKenzie Story
- Beyond the Shadows
- Hell Hath No Fury